Boo!

Halloween Poems and Limericks

Patricia Hubbell

illustrations by Jeff Spackman

MARSHALL CAVENDISH   NEW YORK

Marshall Cavendish Corporation, 99 White Plains Road, Tarrytown, New York 10591

Library of Congress Cataloging-in-Publication Data
Hubbell, Patricia.
Boo! : Halloween poems and limericks / written by Patricia Hubbell ; illustrated by Jeff Spackman.
1st edition   p.   cm.
Summary: A collection of limericks and other poems about Halloween, including "Halloween Scarecrow," "There Once Was a Witch from North Dublin," and "Pumpkin Surprise."
ISBN 0-7614-5023-8
1. Halloween—Juvenile poetry. 2. Children's poetry, American. 3. Limericks, Juvenile. [1. Halloween—Poetry. 2. Limericks. 3. American poetry.] I. Spackman, Jeff, ill. II. Title.
PS3558.U22B66 1998 811'.54—dc21 97-25428 CIP AC

The text of this book is set in 14 point Slimbach Bold.
The illustrations are rendered in acrylics.
Printed in Italy
1 3 5 6 4 2
First edition

For Maron and Charles Lieb
And in memory of Marge Farian and Billie Martin
—Thanks for great Halloweens!
—P.H.

For my nieces and nephews
—J.S.

Contents

Who Is There?

Knock! Knock!
Knock! Knock!

"Who is knocking at my door?
Who is there?
Who has come flying through the air?

"Who is that
All dressed in black
Wearing a tall pointed hat?
Tapping,
Tapping,
At my door,
With her broomstick
At my door?

"Who is that
With a squalling wild-eyed cat?

"Mercy me!
Do not let this creature be
Any relative of ME!"

*"Mother, Mother,
Open wide,
Let your witch child
Come inside!
BOO!"*

7

Cat Curfew

Call the Cats in!
Call the Cats in!
It's Halloween night,
so call your Cats in!

If Cats stay outside
they may beg for a ride
to the dark of the moon
on the old witch's broom!

They may sail up to Mars!
They may roam through the stars!
They may never come home!

They will fly with the bats
and wear masks and black hats.
They will learn to cast spells
and the future foretell.

They'll grow horrible fur!
They'll forget how to purr!
Weird, monsterish, and wild,
they will scare every child!

It's Halloween night, so
CALL YOUR CATS IN!

Halloween Scarecrow

I grew a fat pumpkin,
I painted his face—
He ran through my garden
In leafy green lace.

I put that fat pumpkin
On top of a post
And told him to scare off
The Halloween Ghost.

Next morning, that pumpkin
Was gone from the post—
And slouched on the top
Was the Halloween Ghost!

Who Has Seen the Witch?

(With apologies to C. R.)

Who has seen the Witch?
Neither you nor I,
But when the children
Hide their heads,
The Witch is passing by.

Who has seen the Witch?
Neither I nor you,
But when the dogs
Lie low and moan,
The Witch is passing through.

A Cauldron of Limericks

A tap on the window at night . . .
The dark is a terrible sight . . .
You hear a loud howl,
Then *you* start to yowl,
As your mother turns on the porch light. . . ! . . ! . !!

In the dark of the night—eerie sounds!
Deep moans, like the baying of hounds!
Let us flee! Let us flee!
Let the fastest be *me*—
For the graveyard holds ten heaving mounds!

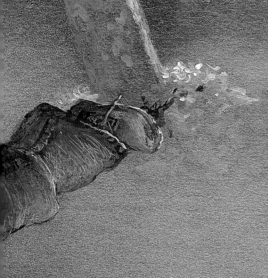

A Ghoul on a grave in West Ruule
Said: "I feel like a terrible fool—
This grave that I'm robbing
Has set me to sobbing,
Which breaks every rule of ghoul school."

A Skeleton who lived in Schenectady
Said: "I feel like a terrible wreck-ta-dy.
My joints are all aching,
My bones are all breaking,
And I fear I've become unconnected-y."

There once was a Witch from North Dublin
Whose troubles kept doublin' and doublin'—
Her best broomstick broke,
Her hat turned to smoke,
Her cauldron refused to get bubblin'.

A Ghost from the town of LaFrance
Taught a Goblin named Rosie to dance.
As they waltzed to and fro
He trod on her toe
Which ended their budding romance.

Squeaked a timid young Bat from Peru—
"Oh, please, tell me *what* shall I do?
The moon is so bright
It gives me a fright,
And the stars are quite worrisome, too!"

On the night when Witches ride high,
The Blorks float and flit through the sky—
Blorks bite and Blorks nip
Until blood starts to drip—

A Goblin who lived in East Weir
Had a curious sort of a fear—
What he feared was just EYES
—Every sort, every size—
Far away, closer by, or QUITE NEAR.

On Halloween

When witches fly
The midnight sky
And black cats howl
And bats zoom by,
I become a stately Queen,
With golden crown and velvet cape,
With sparkling jewels and spangled lace
   (The real *me* I've tried to find
   All my plainness left behind.)
As I pass by, with regal airs,
Everyone just stares and stares.

Pumpkin Surprise

I was picking a pumpkin,
A fat orange pumpkin,
When I spotted a hole
In its side,
A hole like a door,
(A little round door)
A door that led straight
To a house.
In the space of a minute
I saw what was in it—
It wasn't a thing you'd forget—
For curled in that pumpkin,
That plain orange pumpkin,
Was a fat little, gray little *mouse!*
A mouse in a house in a pumpkin!
On a floor that was covered with seeds,
All curled up and cozy,
Snoozy and dozy,
Asleep on a soft bed of weeds!

Halloween Diner

I went down to the diner.
I ordered scrambled eggs.
I peeked beneath the counter—
    Who owns those scrawny legs?
I peeked into the kitchen—
    I saw a tall black hat!
    I think I saw the soup tureen
    disgorge a big black bat!

My scrambled eggs were runny,
They tasted very queer—
    I thought I saw a slimy snake
    slithering quite near!

I pushed my plate away from me.
I ordered apple pie.
    I'm sure I saw a wisp of smoke
    and heard a ghostly sigh!

My apple pie was horrid—
  I think the fruit was slugs.
  I'm sure the drink they served to me
  was cold puree of bugs!

I ran out of the diner.
I threw up in a ditch.
And then I saw the flashing sign:
  NEW OWNERS—GHOST AND WITCH

What the Baby Bat
Saw on Halloween

"Little bat,
Little bat,
On the eave of my house,
You with the face
Of a wizened mouse,
Hanging there,
Feet in the air,
What do you see
On this night of fear?"

"I see a black cat riding on a witch's back!
A vampire sucking up a midnight snack!
A ghost in a graveyard writhing on a stone!
A skeleton rattling every bone, bone, bone!
A monster munching mounds of maggoty meat!
—My big brother calling me for trick-or-treat!"

Who?

On this night,
(Blacker than a crow
Or grackle)
Ghosts moan
And witches cackle.

Robots strut. Clowns cavort.
Spacemen float. Dragons snort.
Lions roar. Gargoyles dance.
Monsters lurch. Skeletons prance.

Now frightened owls from their shadowed perch
Shiver and hoot: "Who-who? Who-who?"

You look at me.
I look at you.
And, like those owls, we ask: "Who?" "Who?"

Bones

Bones
Bones
Clatter
Of bones

Cold wind
Blowing
And a clatter
Of bones

Bones
Bones
Clatter
Of bones

Night owl
Hooting
And the clatter
Of bones

Bones
Bones
Clatter
Of bones

I'm whirling,
Twirling,
To the clatter
Of bones

Gone! Gone!
Where have I gone?
Who will hear me
In this clatter of bones?

Bones
Bones
Clatter
Of bones

Who will find me
In this batch of bones?

The Search

A fussy Witch
who lost her broom
set out to find a new one—

"I hate to be a fussy Witch,"
  the old Witch sighed,
"but I really need a *perfect* broom
  for sailing through the skies—
  a long broom
  a strong broom
  a broom with magic powers
  a fright broom
  a *flight* broom
  a broom for midnight hours."

She searched the malls and grocery stores,
department stores (each floor).
She searched the craft and antique shops
and then she searched some more.

Finding *nothing* maddened her
(and feeling mean and meaner)
she stalked into a hardware store,
one run by Martian giants,
and bought herself a rocket ship—
That nifty new appliance!

The Phantom Squirrel

I wonder
if this gray squirrel
wrapped in silver fog
thinks that he's invisible,
crouched upon his log?

I wonder
when he glides about
from tree to tree to tree,
if he thinks that he's a GHOST
scaring me?

Witch's Brew

Cauldron, Cauldron,
Bubbly hot,
Ask a witch—
Or ask her not—
What she stirs there
By the fire.

Dare to ask,
She'll tell you true
(No witch lives
Who is a liar.)

"I stir toadstools,
Fire ash,
Wind of storm,
Lightning flash,

"Thunderclap,
Rain and hail,
One greeny-pinkish slippery scale
From a dragon's slashing tail,

"Drop of monster blood,
Hen teeth,
Wreath
Of goldenrod and heather,
Ten pints of the foulest weather.

"This recipe, I swear, is true—
And now, it needs a pinch of . . . YOU!"

Tricksters

Tie the gate!
Hide the cow!
Tricksters!
Tricksters!
Coming *now!*

Guard the pigpen,
Guard the house,
Tricksters!
Tricksters!
Getting close!

Lock the chickens
In the coop,
Tricksters!
Tricksters!
On the stoop!

Get the candy!
Get some more!
Tricksters!
Tricksters!
At the door!

Give them all
That they can eat—
Tricksters!
Tricksters!
Turn them sweet!

33

Pumpkins Little, Pumpkins Big

Pumpkins little, pumpkins big,
Pumpkins feed a hungry pig.
A pumpkin makes a mouse's bed
Or a strawman's scary head.

To grow some pumpkins, make a mound
Of crumbly earth on crumbly ground.
Push in three pumpkin seeds.
Water them and wait until
From each flat seed
Two tiny leaves uncurl.

Water. Weed. Wait some more.
Soon, pumpkin vines unfurl.
Then, blossoms gold unfold.
When blossoms fade, pumpkins grow—
And grow some more—
And grow—and GROW!

Soon, we're making pumpkin pies
And carving pumpkin mouths and eyes.
Now, pumpkin clowns and spooky spies
And pumpkins in a witch disguise
Watch the great moon slowly rise
As candles light their eyes.

Pumpkins, pumpkins, everywhere!
At the farm, at the fair,
On the porch, on the stair,
Riding broomsticks in the air,
Hogging Grandpa's rocking chair—
Jack-o'-lanterns everywhere!

Halloween Alphabet

A for Attics. Awed. Afraid. Apples in a tub.

B for Bobbing. Bats. Brooms. BOO!

C for Cats and Creepy.

D for Doughnuts. Devils. Dark.

E for EEEEEEK! And Eerie.

F for Fright and Fear and Flee.

G for Ghosts and Goblins.

H for Hats and Haunt and Help!

I for poor old Me.

J for Jack-o'-lantern. Jump. Jump, jump, jump away!

K for Knock, and Keep me safe.

L for Let me be!

M for Monsters, Moans, and Masks. Moon and Mischief. Magic.

N for Nightmares. No! No! No! Night as dark as pitch.

O for Oh! Just Oh! Oh! Oh! Ohhhhhhhhh! I saw a witch!

P for Pumpkins, Plain and carved.

Q for Quiet! Quaking!

R for Rats and Rattle. ROOOOOOAAAAR! Rap, rap, rap,
    upon the door.

S for Scared. Shudder. Shake. Screams and Shivery
Shadows.

T for Trick or Treat, and Trolls.

U for Ugh! Up there!

V for Vampires and for Vats, and Very,
    Very shaky.

W for Werewolf, Wizard, Whoooooooooosh!
    Witch, and Who? What? Where?

X for eXtra scared. That's me.

Y for You are, too.

Z for ZZZZZZZZZZZZ. Home safe.
    Home free. Curled in bed.
    Asleep.
    ZZZZZZZZZZZZZZZZ!

The Old House on Halloween

On Halloween,
    the old house
        moans and groans and sighs,
remembering the children,
from days gone by.

On Halloween,
    the old house
        shivers in its sleep,
thinking how the ghosts and
the goblins used to creep.

On Halloween,
    the old house
        laughs a rueful laugh,
thinking how its windows
(with their bubbled glass)
used to watch the children,
flapping in old sheets—
How the children bobbed for apples,
and pulled taffy treats.

On Halloween,
    the old house
        settles on its bones,
listens to October's wind
crying in the tree—
    *"Children, children, everywhere,
        but not one for me."*

The Unicorn

Whenever
I see a Unicorn,
I remind myself—
    One has never been born—

This
beautiful beast
with the
delicate horn

lives
in mythology,
not
in zoology.

They're make-believe.
They're just pretend.
No, they're *not* a thing
you can really befriend.

So why does my heart
grow glad and light,
when I see one prancing
on Halloween night?